CUT & ASSEMBLE

VICTORIAN HOUSES

Four Full-Color Buildings in H-O Scale

Edmund V. Gillon Jr.

Dover Publications, Inc.
New York

Copyright © 1979 by Dover Publications, Inc.
All rights reserved under Pan American and International Copyright Conventions.

Published in Canada by General Publishing Company, Ltd., 30 Lesmill Road, Don Mills, Toronto, Ontario.
Published in the United Kingdom by Constable and Company, Ltd., 10 Orange Street, London WC2H 7EG.

Cut & Assemble Victorian Houses is a new work, first published by Dover Publications, Inc., in 1979.

International Standard Book Number: 0-486-23849-0
Library of Congress Catalog Card Number: 79-53312

Manufactured in the United States of America
Dover Publications, Inc.
180 Varick Street
New York, N.Y. 10014

Introduction and Instructions

The Victorian era of American architecture stretches across the last half of the nineteenth century. The style is found throughout the country, from the New England states to the West Coast.

Victorian domestic architecture is extremely eclectic and ornamental, borrowing freely from previous stylistic periods to form pictorial compositions. The houses are characteristically tall with great contrast in color and texture of building materials; they are often embellished with belvederes, cupolas, dormers, porticos and ornate iron- and woodwork.

The houses in this book are distinct examples of some of the most popular Victorian styles. The Second Empire and stick style houses are based on diagrams and plans in A. J. Bicknell's *Village Builder and Supplement* (New York: A. J. Bicknell, 1878; reprinted by Dover under the title *Bicknell's Victorian Buildings: Floor Plans and Elevations for 45 Houses and Other Structures*).

The Octagon house was popular before the Civil War and became widely known through the book *A Home for All or the Gravel Wall and Octagon Mode of Building*, by Orson Squire Fowler. Fowler considered the octagon a more advantageous living space since the eight-sided shape provided more square feet of floor area than the traditional rectangular house. The usually flat roof of this type house often is surmounted by a belvedere.

Characteristic of the stick style house are steep roofs and accentuated wooden frames and brackets. The decorative framing seems almost a continuation of the basic structure. This type of house is considered a distinctly American style. Whereas many Victorian styles were adapted for various types of buildings, the stick style is found basically in country residences and small churches and chapels.

The Second Empire style receives its name from the French Second Empire (the reign of Napoleon III, 1852–1870). One of the first examples was the extension of the Palace of the Louvre, called the New Louvre. The Paris Opera House is another superb Second Empire building. In its most ornate form, it was a popular American style for public buildings as demonstrated by the Boston and Philadelphia city halls. It also become a favorite style in

domestic architecture. Characteristic of this type house are the mansard roof and dormer window.

The Italianate villa style is an imitation of the architecture of Italian farmhouses. Though most widely used for picturesque private residences, some public buildings have been designed in this mode. Asymmetrical design, slightly pitched roofs, balconies and towers were inherent in its construction. Most often the Italianate villa was built of stone.

GENERAL DIRECTIONS:

The recommended tools to construct these houses are: 1) an X-acto knife with a #11 blade, 2) water-soluble white glue, such as Elmer's or Sobo, and 3) a scoring tool. A burnishing tool for applying pressure to glued joints and a straightedge for scoring and cutting are also suggested.

Carefully and accurately cut out all pieces needed for a given structure. These are numbered and identified by code letters on a glue tab. Never cut out any areas within a piece unless they are marked with an "X" or the words "Cut Out." Some areas so marked are merely to facilitate gluing; others are for decorative effects.

All glue tabs are indicated with a dot. Apply glue to only the tab itself, never to the receiving surface. Do not apply too much glue—it will seep out and mar the printed surface. Allow each glued joint to dry completely before further handling. Bracket and porch-post tabs not marked with glue dots can be glued to insure their staying in place. Those that have no tabs can be anchored in place with a drop of glue.

Study the photographs and exploded diagrams to see how pieces fit together. Also read the special instructions accompanying the diagrams. For neater and more accurate results, score along all fold lines before folding. Broken or dashed lines indicate folds that might not be obvious.

The areas on roofs not marked with shingles are for the placement of chimneys and dormers.

Please note that all stairway units must be cut along the horizontal lines from the tabs to the fold line. There is also a small piece with one or more triangular tabs to be attached to the base. The triangular tabs are folded in and the stair treads glued on to complete the stairway.

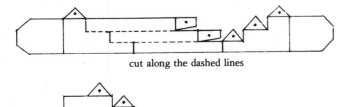

cut along the dashed lines

glue this piece to larger unit and fold triangles over

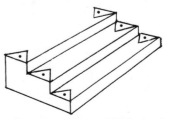

glue step treads onto folded triangles

CUT & ASSEMBLE
VICTORIAN HOUSES

OCTAGON HOUSE

This house consists of 35 pieces keyed OH on Plates A–C. Piece OH-19 refers to all 24 cornice brackets which are inserted in slots cut through the walls. Pieces OH-11–OH-13 (the back overhanging porch) and OH-14–OH-18 (the back stairway unit) are assembled and attached in the same manner as the front porch and steps. OH-8 (not pictured) is part of the front stairway unit. (See general directions for stairway unit construction.) The roof and walls should be assembled separately and then put together only after the glue on both units has been allowed to dry thoroughly.

Text continues after the Plates

CUT & ASSEMBLE
VICTORIAN HOUSES

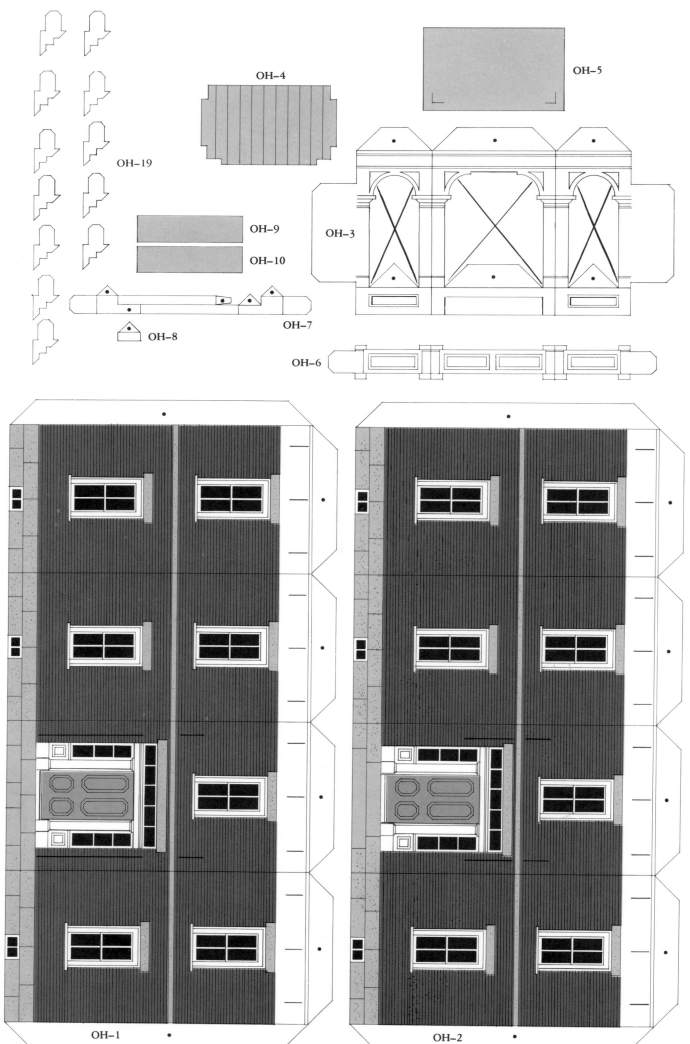

OH–4

OH–5

OH–19

OH–9

OH–10

OH–3

OH–7

OH–8

OH–6

OH–1

OH–2

Plate A

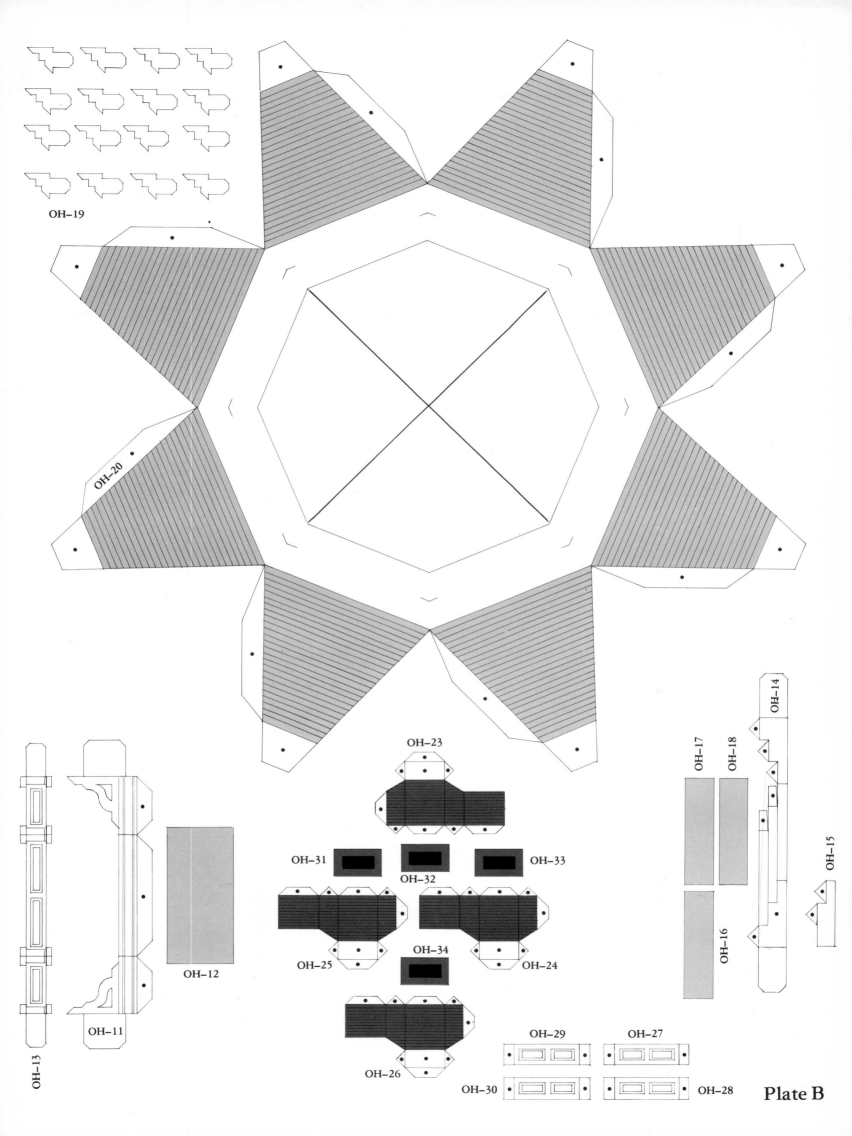

OH–19

OH–20

OH–13

OH–11

OH–12

OH–23

OH–31

OH–32

OH–33

OH–25

OH–24

OH–34

OH–26

OH–29

OH–27

OH–30

OH–28

OH–17

OH–18

OH–14

OH–15

OH–16

Plate B

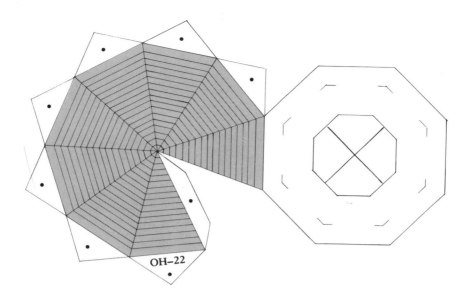

OH–22

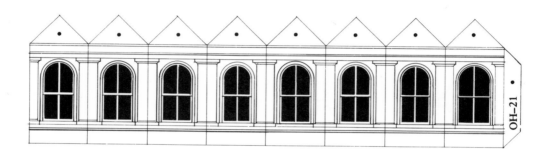

OH–21

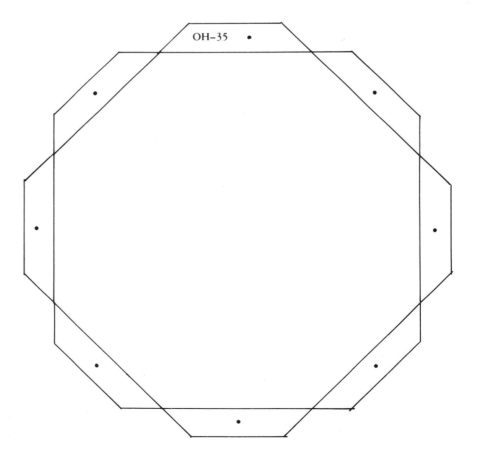

OH–35

Plate C

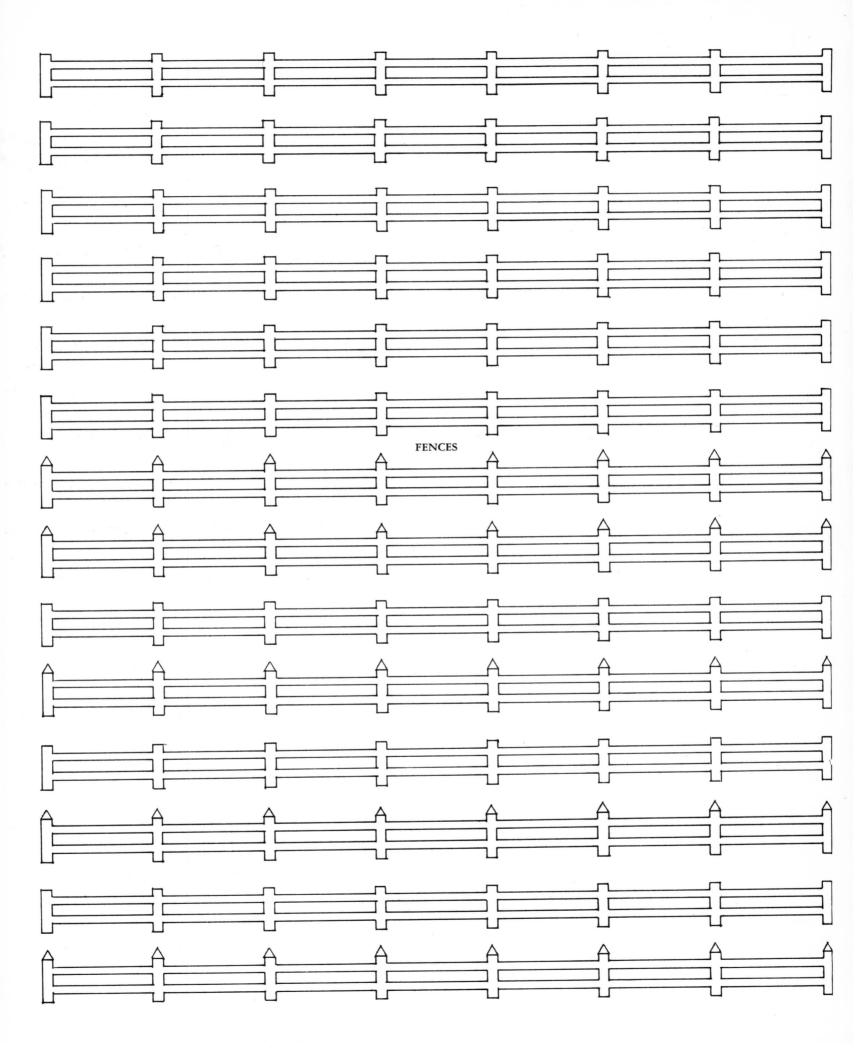

FENCES

Plate D

SE-1

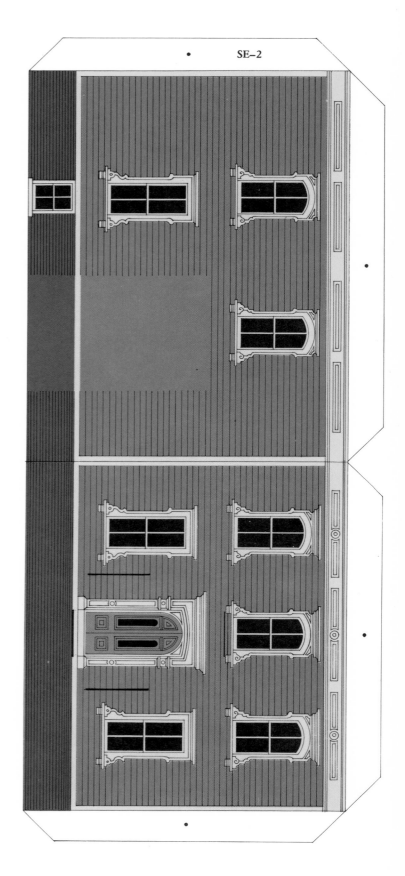

SE-2

Plate E

SE–14   SE–13

SE–12

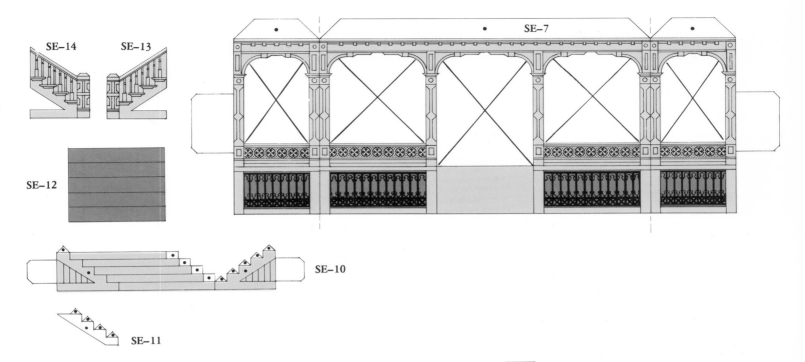

SE–7

SE–10

SE–11

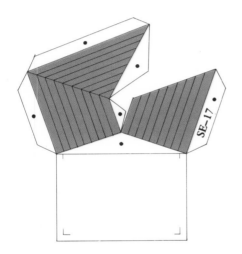

SE–17

SE–40   SE–38

SE–39   SE–37

SE–36   SE–34

SE–35   SS–33

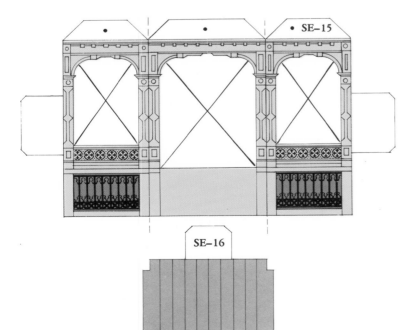

SE–15

SE–16

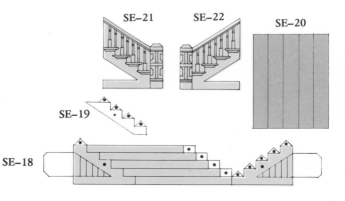

SE–21   SE–22   SE–20

SE–19

SE–18

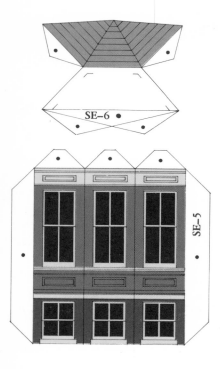

SE–6

SE–5

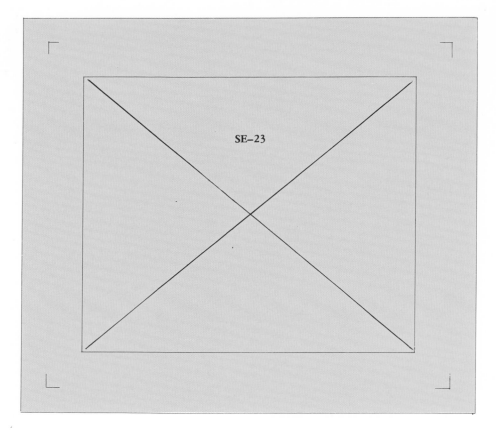

SE–23

SE–8

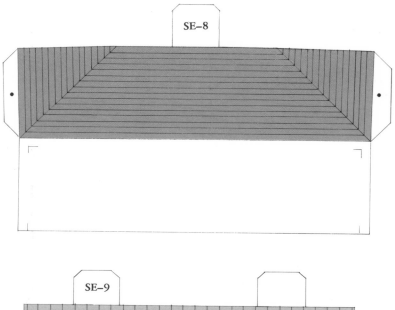

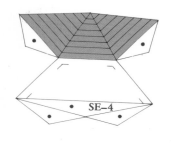

SE–4

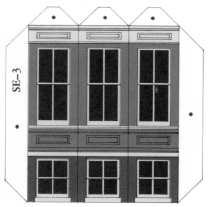

SE–3

SE–9

Plate G

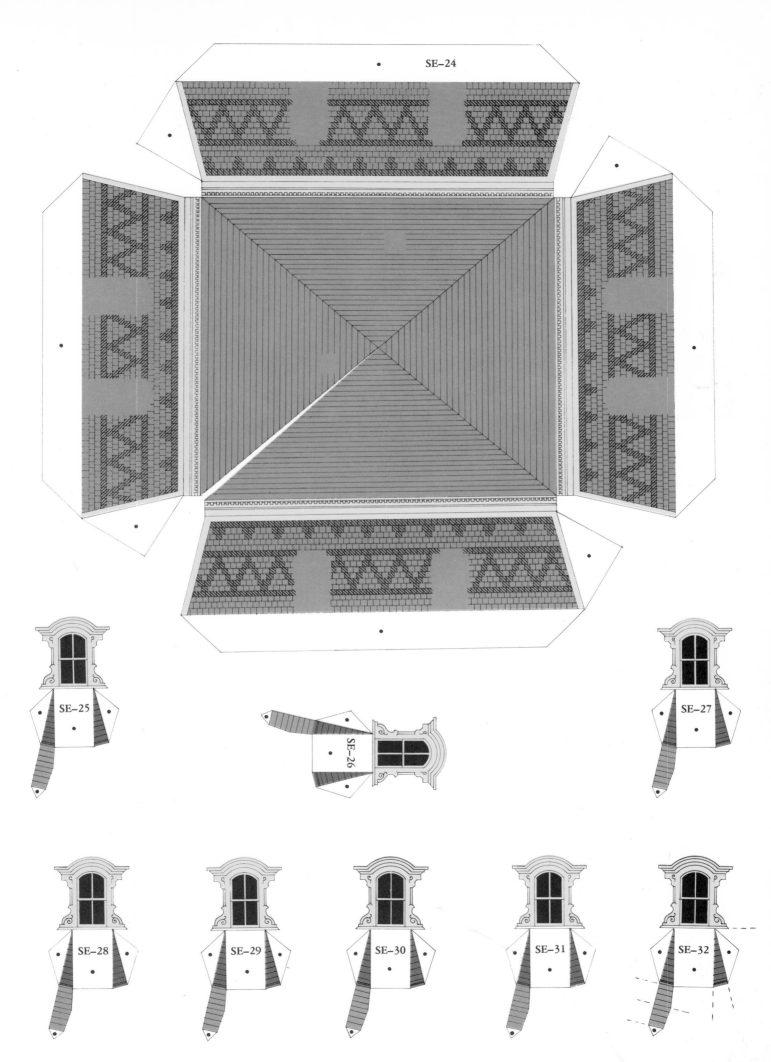

SE–24

SE–25

SE–26

SE–27

SE–28

SE–29

SE–30

SE–31

SE–32

Plate H

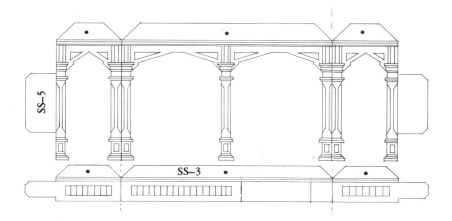

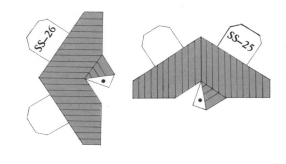

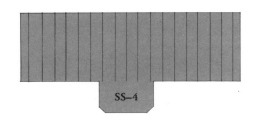

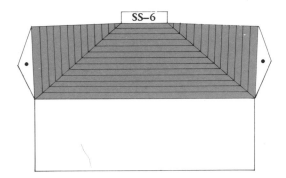

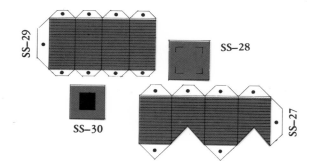

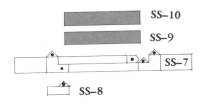

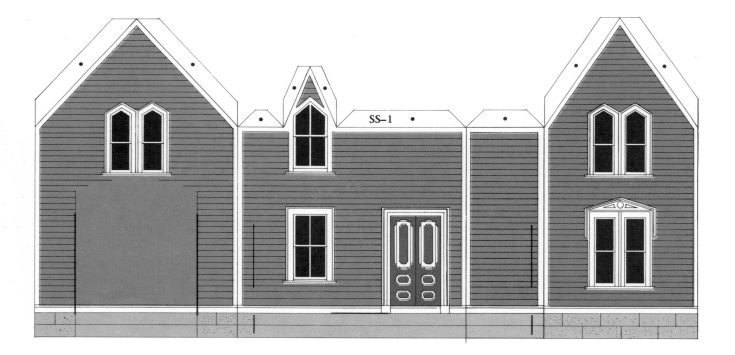

Plate I

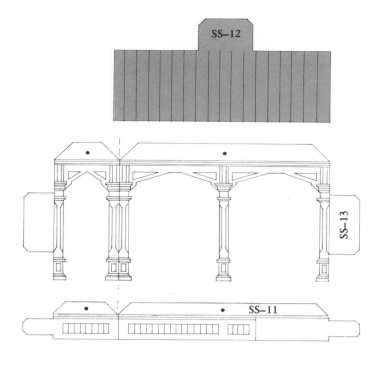

SS–12

SS–13

SS–11

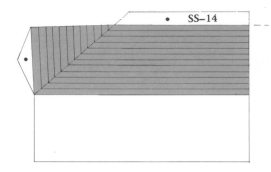

SS–14

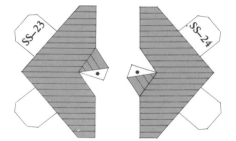

SS–23

SS–24

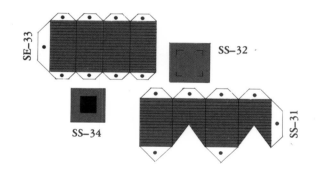

SE–33

SS–32

SS–34

SS–31

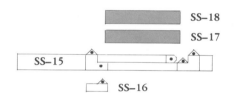

SS–18

SS–17

SS–15

SS–16

SS–2

Plate J

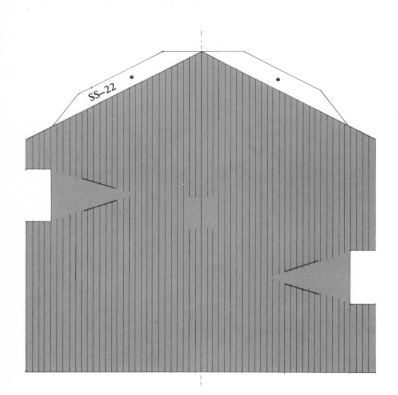

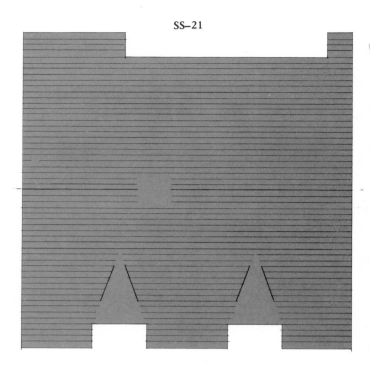

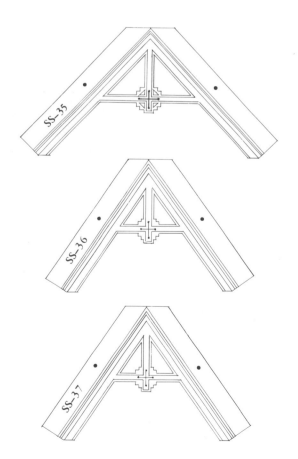

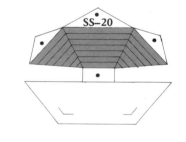

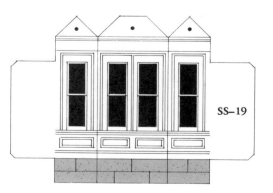

Plate K

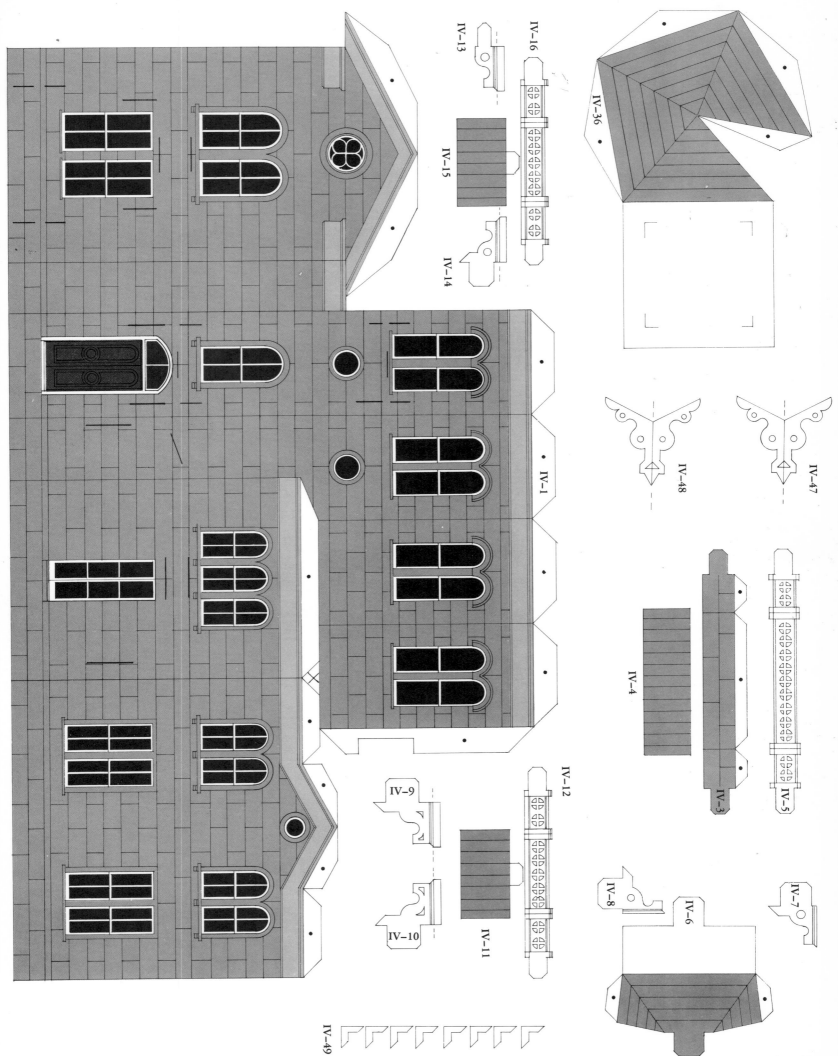

IV-13

IV-16

IV-15

IV-14

IV-36

IV-1

IV-48

IV-47

IV-4

IV-3

IV-5

IV-9

IV-12

IV-10

IV-11

IV-8

IV-6

IV-7

IV-49

Plate L

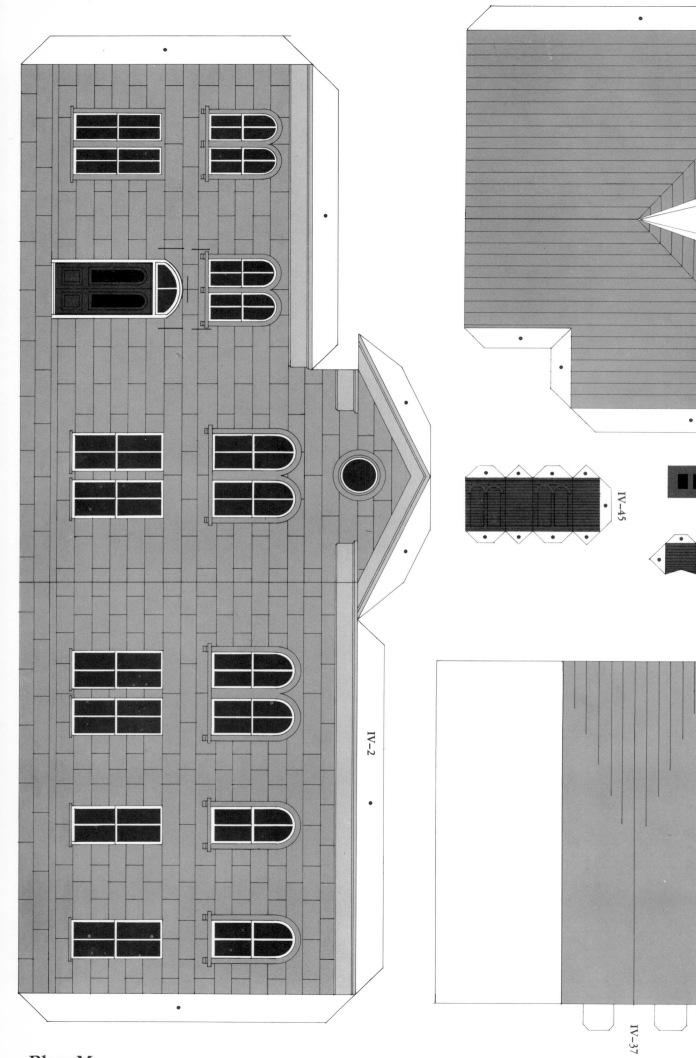

Plate M

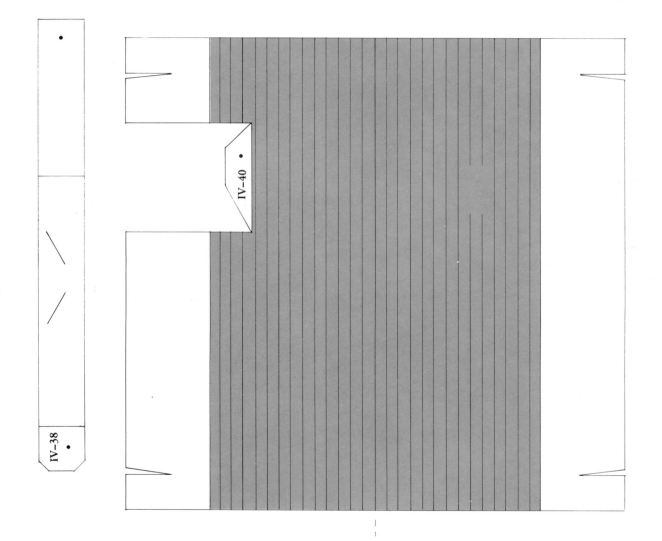

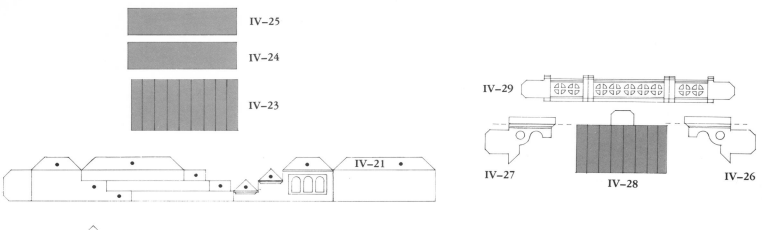

IV–25

IV–24

IV–23

IV–29

IV–27

IV–28

IV–26

IV–21

IV–22

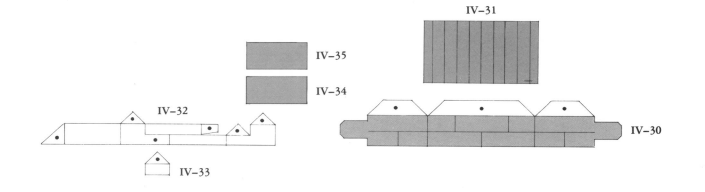

IV–31

IV–35

IV–34

IV–32

IV–33

IV–30

IV–42

IV–20

IV–41

IV–19

IV–18

IV–17

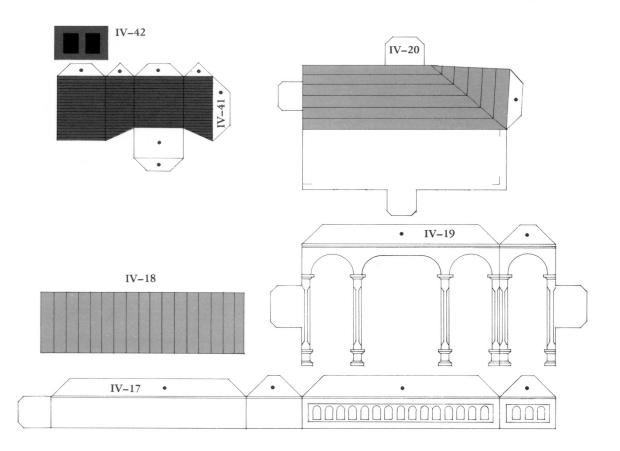

Plate O

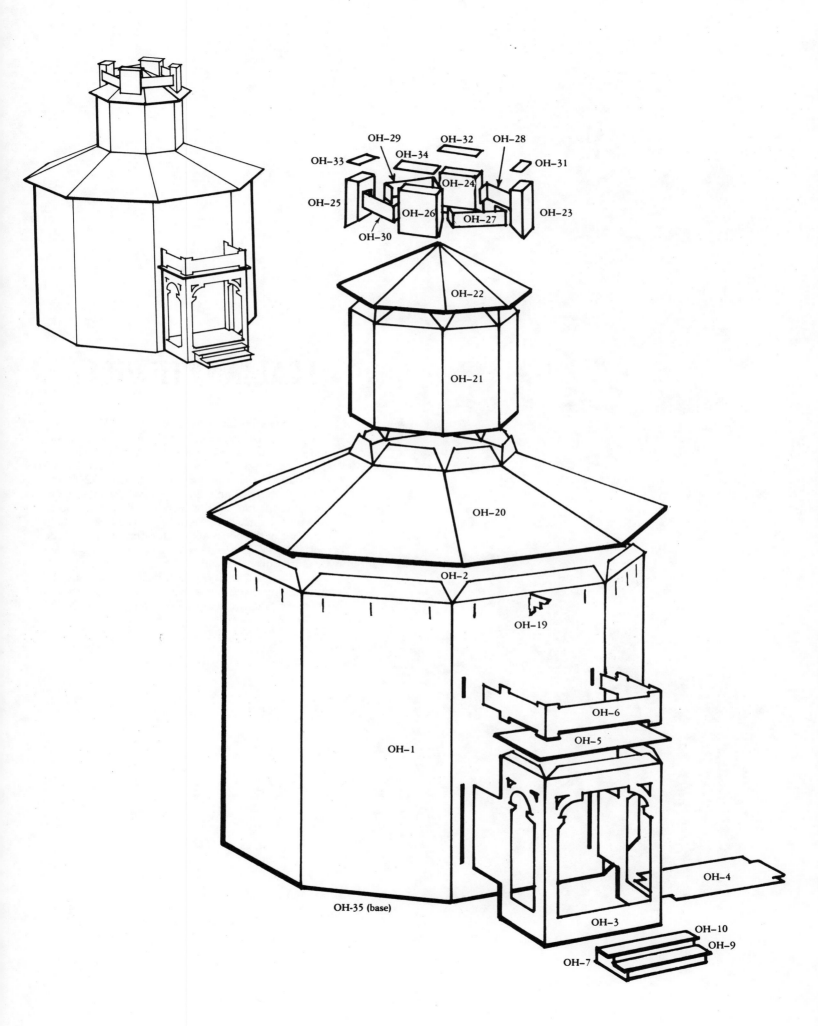

OH–29 OH–32 OH–28

OH–33 OH–34 OH–31

OH–25 OH–24

OH–26 OH–23

OH–30 OH–27

OH–22

OH–21

OH–20

OH–2

OH–19

OH–6

OH–5

OH–1

OH–4

OH–3

OH–10

OH–35 (base) OH–9

OH–7

9

ITALIANATE VILLA

The villa consists of 49 pieces keyed IV on Plates L–O. IV-22 (not pictured) is part of the front stairway unit. (See general directions for stairway unit construction.) Pieces IV-26–IV-29 (the back balcony), IV-30 and IV-31 (the back porch) and IV-32–IV-35 (the back stairway unit) are assembled and attached in the same manner as the corresponding front pieces shown in the diagram. Piece IV-38 is a brace to hold the shape of the house and anchor the first part of the roof. Piece IV-49 refers to all 8 cornice brackets which are glued under the eaves of the roof, four to each side. This house has an eaved roof; in order to create the overhanging eaves, cut along the lines of the roof to where the house is folded for corners (pieces IV-1 and IV-2).

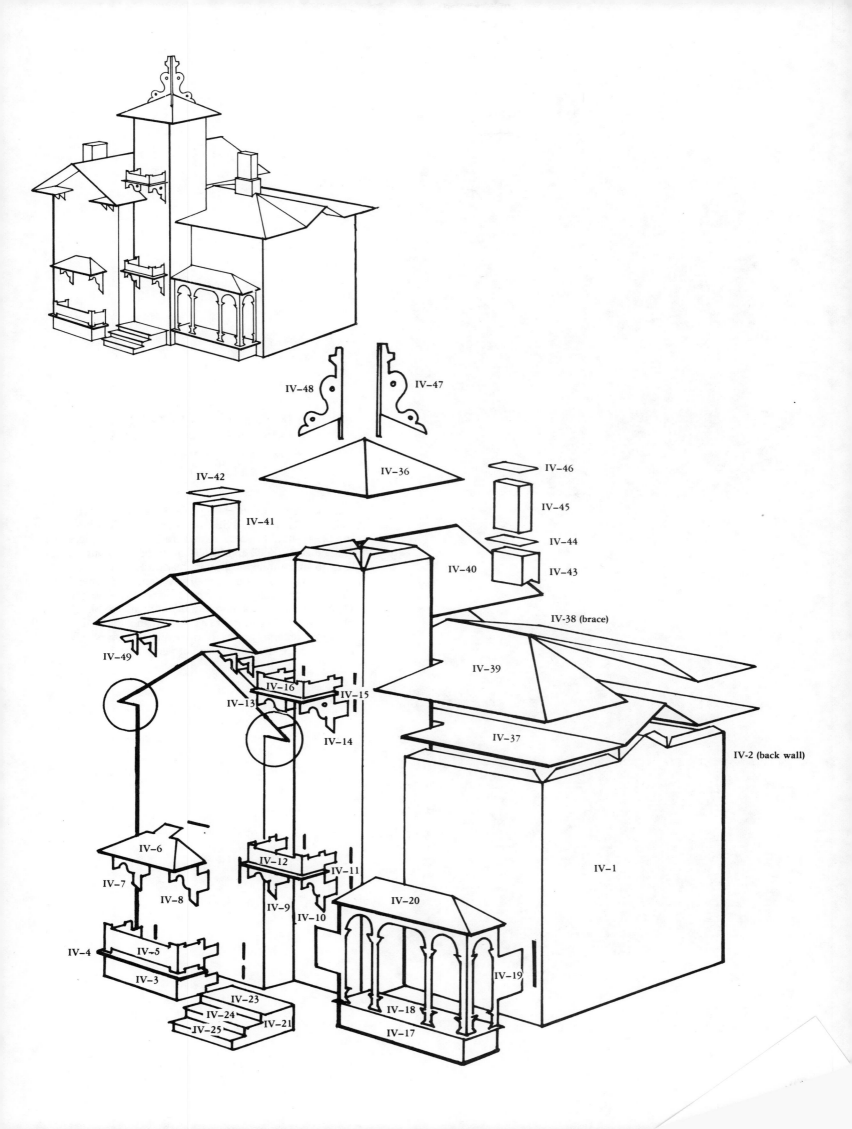

IV–48   IV–47

IV–42   IV–36   IV–46

IV–41   IV–45

IV–44

IV–40   IV–43

IV–38 (brace)

IV–49   IV–39

IV–16   IV–37   IV–2 (back wall)

IV–13   IV–15

IV–14

IV–6   IV–12   IV–11

IV–7   IV–1

IV–8   IV–9   IV–10

IV–20

IV–4   IV–5

IV–3   IV–19

IV–23   IV–18

IV–24   IV–21

IV–25   IV–17

SECOND EMPIRE HOUSE

This house consists of 40 pieces keyed SE on Plates E–H. Pieces SE-5 and SE-6, a bay window like SE-3 and SE-4, should be attached where indicated on piece SE-2. Pieces SE-12 and SE-20 are to be cut along all lines to make individual stair treads. SE-11 (not pictured) is part of the front stairway unit. (See general directions for stairway unit construction.) Pieces SE-15–SE-17 (the back porch unit) and SE-18–SE-22 (the back stairway unit) are assembled and attached in the same manner as the front porch and stairs. SE-29–SE-32 are the other four dormers.

SE–40
SE–39
SE–38
SE–37

SE–36
SE–35
SE–34
SE–33

SE–28
SE–27
SE–24
SE–26
SE–25
SE–23

SE–2

SE–1

SE–4
SE–8
SE–7
SE–3

SE–9

SE–13
SE–12
SE–14
SE–10

STICK STYLE HOUSE

This house consists of 37 pieces keyed SS on Plates I–K. Pieces SS-7–SS-10 constitute the back stairway unit that is attached to SS-3. SS-16 (not pictured) is part of the front stairway unit. (See general directions for stairway unit construction.) SS-24, SS-25 and SS-26 are dormers identical to SS-23. SS-37 is a frame like SS-35.

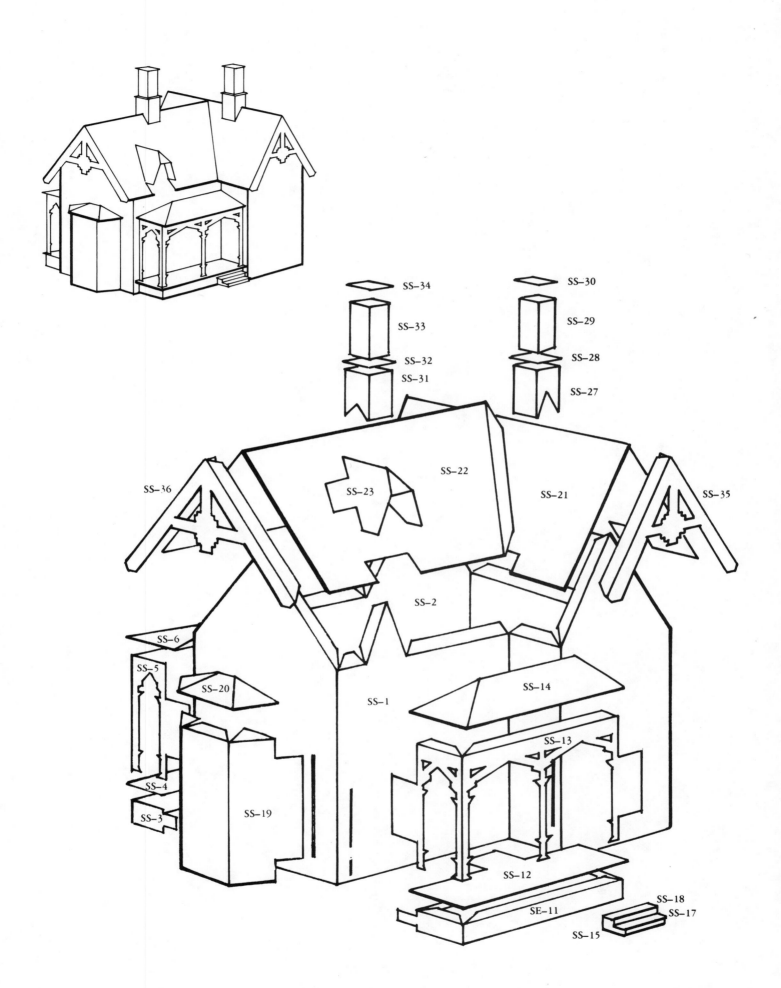

SS–34

SS–30

SS–33

SS–29

SS–32

SS–28

SS–31

SS–27

SS–36

SS–22

SS–23

SS–21

SS–35

SS–2

SS–6

SS–5

SS–14

SS–20

SS–1

SS–13

SS–4

SS–3

SS–19

SS–12

SE–11

SS–18

SS–17

SS–15